CELEBRATING THE CITY OF BUENOS AIRES

Celebrating the City of Buenos Aires

Walter the Educator

SKB
Silent King Books

Copyright © 2024 by Walter the Educator

All rights reserved. No part of this book may be reproduced in any manner whatsoever without written per- mission except in the case of brief quotations embodied in critical articles and reviews.

First Printing, 2024

Disclaimer

This book is a literary work; the story is not about specific persons, locations, situations, and/or circumstances unless mentioned in a historical context. Any resemblance to real persons, locations, situations, and/or circumstances is coincidental. This book is for entertainment and informational purposes only. The author and publisher offer this information without warranties expressed or implied. No matter the grounds, neither the author nor the publisher will be accountable for any losses, injuries, or other damages caused by the reader's use of this book. The use of this book acknowledges an understanding and acceptance of this disclaimer.

Celebrating the City of Buenos Aires is a little collectible souvenir book that belongs to the Celebrating Cities Book Series by Walter the Educator. Collect them all and more books at WaltertheEducator.com

USE THE EXTRA SPACE TO TAKE NOTES AND DOCUMENT YOUR MEMORIES

BUENOS AIRES

In Buenos Aires, where the tango's hum,
Celebrating the City of Buenos Aires

The streets, a melody, a vibrant drum,

A city crafted from dreams and sighs,

Underneath the wide, expansive skies.

The Río de la Plata whispers tales,

Of sailors' journeys and ships' proud sails,

Where cultures blend in a passionate dance,

Celebrating the City of Buenos Aires

In the heart of the city, love finds its chance.

La Boca bursts in a colorful spree,

With hues that splash in wild decree,

Corrugated homes in bright array,

Artists' haven, come what may.

Caminito's path, a painted stretch,

Where every corner, memories etch,

Tango steps on cobblestone,

In this lively, open-air zone.

Celebrating the City of Buenos Aires

Recoleta, with its marble graves,

Legends rest in its shadowy caves,

Evita sleeps in eternal grace,

A symbol of Argentina's face.

San Telmo breathes with antique charm,

Markets bustling, arm in arm,

Cobblestone whispers of days long past,

Histories woven, deep and vast.

Palermo's parks, green and serene,

Celebrating the City of Buenos Aires

A city's lungs, pure and clean,

Botanic gardens with flowers rare,

A peaceful haven, beyond compare.

Avenida 9 de Julio wide,

The world's broadest, in stride,

Obelisco stands tall and proud,

A sentinel among the crowd.

Cafés buzz with a friendly cheer,

Yerba mate shared, sincere,
Celebrating the City of Buenos Aires

Conversations, deep and bright,

Echo through the city's night.

So raise a glass, let spirits sing,

In Buenos Aires, joy takes wing,

For in its heart, we find our own,

A place where dreams are brightly sown.

ABOUT THE CREATOR

Walter the Educator is one of the pseudonyms for Walter Anderson. Formally educated in Chemistry, Business, and Education, he is an educator, an author, a diverse entrepreneur, and he is the son of a disabled war veteran. "Walter the Educator" shares his time between educating and creating. He holds interests and owns several creative projects that entertain, enlighten, enhance, and educate, hoping to inspire and motivate you. Follow, find new works, and stay up to date with Walter the Educator™ at WaltertheEducator.com

Milton Keynes UK
Ingram Content Group UK Ltd.
UKHW020101050824
446426UK00013B/251

CELEBRATING THE CITY OF CHIBA

Celebrating the City of Chiba

Walter the Educator

SKB
Silent King Books

Copyright © 2024 by Walter the Educator

All rights reserved. No part of this book may be reproduced in any manner whatsoever without written per- mission except in the case of brief quotations embodied in critical articles and reviews.

First Printing, 2024

Disclaimer

This book is a literary work; the story is not about specific persons, locations, situations, and/or circumstances unless mentioned in a historical context. Any resemblance to real persons, locations, situations, and/or circumstances is coincidental. This book is for entertainment and informational purposes only. The author and publisher offer this information without warranties expressed or implied. No matter the grounds, neither the author nor the publisher will be accountable for any losses, injuries, or other damages caused by the reader's use of this book. The use of this book acknowledges an understanding and acceptance of this disclaimer.

Celebrating the City of Chiba is a little collectible souvenir book that belongs to the Celebrating Cities Book Series by Walter the Educator. Collect them all and more books at WaltertheEducator.com

USE THE EXTRA SPACE TO TAKE NOTES AND DOCUMENT YOUR MEMORIES

CHIBA

In the embrace of Chiba's gentle shores,

Celebrating the City of Chiba

Where the sun spills gold on silken floors,

The whispering wind through emerald leaves,

Echoes tales of dreams, where the heart believes.

Oh, Chiba, cradle of ancient lore,

With each sunrise, I adore you more.

From Makuhari's bustling streets alive,

To Narita's gateways where dreams arrive.

Your gardens bloom with sakura blush,

In spring's embrace, a quiet hush.

Celebrating the City of
Chiba

Boso's fields, a tapestry of green,

Where farmers toil, and nature's seen.

The ocean's song by Kujukuri's sand,

A melody composed by nature's hand.

Fishermen's nets, a silvery gleam,

In dawn's first light, a tranquil dream.

Oh, Chiba, city of a thousand hues,

Your spirit, a canvas, the artist's muse.

From Choshi's lighthouse, the morning's glow,

Celebrating the City of Chiba

To sawara's streets where rivers flow.

Yoro Valley, where the waters play,

In a symphony of night and day.

Temples that touch the sky's embrace,

With whispered prayers, a sacred space.

Kimitsu's forests, a realm so fair,

With hidden trails and perfumed air.

Mother Farm, where children's laughter rings,

In fields where every blossom sings.

Celebrating the City of
Chiba

Chiba, your essence, a poem in flight,

A tapestry woven with threads of light.

In each corner, a story unfolds,

Of courage, honor, and hearts of gold.

The echoes of warriors from ages past,

In your soil, their legacies cast.

Kisarazu's bridges, a testament of steel,

Spanning the waters with a future to reveal.

Oh, Chiba, with every dawn anew,

Celebrating the City of Chiba

In your arms, the dreams accrue.

With every step, a path unknown,

In your heart, we find our own.

ABOUT THE CREATOR

Walter the Educator is one of the pseudonyms for Walter Anderson. Formally educated in Chemistry, Business, and Education, he is an educator, an author, a diverse entrepreneur, and he is the son of a disabled war veteran. "Walter the Educator" shares his time between educating and creating. He holds interests and owns several creative projects that entertain, enlighten, enhance, and educate, hoping to inspire and motivate you. Follow, find new works, and stay up to date with Walter the Educator™ at WaltertheEducator.com

Milton Keynes UK
Ingram Content Group UK Ltd.
UKHW020101050824
446426UK00013B/252